LEYLAND FLEET

The Leyland buses of
WIGAN
CORPORATION

by Ron Phillips

THE LEYLAND SOCIETY

Wigan Corporation Tramways

Wigan Corporation commenced electric tramway operation on 25th January 1901, with the route to Martland Mill, but company operated horse and steam tramways had preceded this event. Wigan adopted the narrow gauge (3 feet 6 inches) to match that of the steam trams, which remained under private ownership until purchase by the Corporation. A second route to the Boar's Head (on the road to Standish) was opened on 6th June 1901. The next line consisted of part of what was to be the New Springs route, a mile long section to Scholes, opened on 21st December 1901. It reached New Springs on 16th May 1902, when short extensions were also made at Martland Mill and Boar's Head. The trams were kept in a "temporary" currogated-iron shed in Woodhouse Lane, Martland Mill.

On 30th September 1902 Wigan Corporation took over operation of the steam tramways from the Wigan & District Tramways Co. Ltd, with routes to Pemberton, Hindley and Platt Bridge. It was decided in March 1903 to electrify the route to Platt Bridge; the work was quickly undertaken and operations by electric car commenced 29th May, 1903, using the existing tracks and the depot at Platt Bridge. This was a most unusual event. Another decision was made in March 1903, partly as a result of local politics, and that was to seek powers to convert all existing and authorised tramways to the standard gauge. These powers were duly conferred in August by the Wigan Corporation Tramways Act, 1903.

The Corporation now altered an order for new cars from narrow to standard gauge. Twelve of the existing narrow-gauge cars were offered for sale, and eventually went to Coventry. A new depot (Central Depot) was planned for standard gauge cars at Melverley Street. During the summer of 1904 the Pemberton route was converted as a standard gauge electric line, and work commenced on the Platt Bridge conversion. Pemberton opened for traffic on 28th July, Platt Bridge on 2nd September after less than a year as a narrow gauge electric route.Also inaugurated on the same day was the first section of track on the Ashton route, which was opened in full on 21st October.

Steam tram operation ceased for good when the Hindley route closed for reconstruction on 26th September 1904.The electric service opened in stages, commencing 7th December 1904. The next section opened on 30th March 1905, together with a loop line on the Ashton service via Poolstock. The trams finally began to run to Hindley again from 4th October 1905. Meanwhile the Boar's Head route was extended to Standish on standard gauge, and the rest of the track was reconstructed, service being restarted on 5th July 1905. Only two more extensions were to come, Pemberton - Abbey Lakes opened 11th April 1906 and New Springs -Aspull (narrow gauge) which opened the following day. Wigan now had almost 24 route miles of tramways, with five and a half route miles still on narrow tracks. There were 13 double deck narrow gauge cars and 54 single deck standard gauge cars.

In 1923 the Aspull route was reconstructed to standard gauge as far as New Springs, the final section being abandoned and operated by Corporation buses. In May

1925 the Martland Mill line was converted to trolleybus operation (see page 12) and the narrow gauge trams were broken up along with their temporary depot, which had stood since 1901.

      The standard gauge tram route to Platt Bridge was taken over by buses in 1927, but the track and wiring remained in situ used by one car a day to preserve the running rights. All the routes were all closed down in 1930-31 in favour of Leyland TD1 buses - the details of which are found on pages 10-11.

SAME PLACE - DIFFERENT GAUGES

Above is the scene in Wigan Lane (the Infirmary), on the Boar's Head route, before the line was extended to Standish and widened to standard gauge. Car 21 is going outwards to Boar's Head on the narrow gauge whilst below single deck car 28 is seen after the 1905 reconstruction to broad gauge.   (Photos courtesy A.K.Kirby)

Early Buses

Wigan Corporation first considered motor bus operation in 1914 in respect of a route from Standish to Coppull, with Commer and Tilling-Stevens buses in mind, but after a visit by the Committee to inspect the roads of the proposed route the idea was dropped. The first buses, two locally made Pagefields, were purchased in 1919. An AEC and six Tilling-Stevens petrol-electrics were placed in service the next year, but financial losses on the buses brought cut-backs in the services and the sale of some of the vehicles at the end of 1922.

Between 1924-1927, seventeen Thornycroft single deckers were purchased as once again bus routes were introduced to serve areas beyond the tramway network. Most were 20 seaters operated by one man. Bus drivers were recruited from existing tramway motormen, and drove both types of vehicle as required. For one man duties, they received an extra halfpenny added to their daily rate. Following the consideration of the future of the Platt Bridge trams, an order was placed for six Bristol B 30-seat buses and three 3-axle 40-seat Karriers, and from 22nd August 1927 buses replaced trams on the Platt Bridge route. A "skeleton" tram service was retained, as the changeover was regarded officially as experimental.

Late in 1927, an order was placed with Leyland for two PLSC1 Lions, with 31 seat bodies. These took fleet numbers 9 and 10, and a third with fleet number 7 was delivered shortly after. These buses with Leyland made bodywork caused the usual furore about the Council not supporting local coach building firms, with the result that several more Bristols and three Pagefields, all bar one with locally made bodywork, joined the fleet in 1928-9. The bus fleet then stood at 37, and the buses carried the fleet numbers 1-37 in a single sequence.

Fleet Numbering

Right from the start, Wigan re-allocated a vacated fleet number to the next new bus. This policy stood throughout the life of the undertaking, and certainly in later times it appeared rather eccentric. No other town did quite the same thing for over fifty years. A complication with this system is that some vehicles, retained for short-term use after their replacements had arrived, carried duplicate numbers. They continued in service with an 'A' suffix to their number, (a practice which was not unique to Wigan.) In the early days, when buses were purchased in small batches, the gap-filling number policy did not seem as odd as it did in later years, when larger batches of buses had numbers scattered about. As the fleet size grew, higher numbers were issued up to 165, with all the lower numbers filled (see, for example, page 31).

In the sixties, the size of the fleet was reduced as a result of falling traffic. The first Atlantean, which was displayed at the Commercial Motor Show, was given the number 166, and thereafter new buses filled in vacant blocks of numbers in the series, so that buses of each distinct type were numbered in a sequential block. Other towns, such as nearby Warrington, numbered buses in this way. Just before Wigan lost its municipal buses, a few vehicles were re-numbered in order to clear a distinct block.

Livery

The numbering scheme was not the only thing which made Wigan buses stand out. The original colour scheme chosen in 1900 for the trams then being built was the same as that in use in Liverpool, crimson lake and cream. This livery was changed in 1913 to carmine red and white, and these were the colours applied to all Wigan buses. On the trams, as was the fashion of the times, the red was lined out with gold and the white was lined out with red. The fleetname and fleet numbers were displayed by shaded gold transfers. The 1913 tramcar livery survived throughout the life of Wigan Corporation Transport with minor modifications, only in the last few years did the newer buses lose the legend "Wigan Corporation" in favour of a much smaller one in unshaded letters reading "County Borough of Wigan". This appeared between decks instead of on the white band above the lower deck windows.Advertising on the exterior of the buses was never allowed, although it did appear on buses still in Wigan livery after take-over by the GMPTE.

As will be seen from the photographs, Wigan buses had white roofs. For a time, they also had white tyres. The picture on page 22 of the breakdown vehicle built from bus No.65 illustrates this feature. It seems to have been introduced in the late thirties, and was particularly appropriate during the Second World War, when buses across the country were also given white edges to the mudguards, and sometimes to rear bumpers and side lifeguards as an aid to visibility during the blackout.

Two Green Lights

Wigan Corporation buses were equipped with two green lights, situated either side of the front indicators. The purpose was to allow the waiting passenger to pick out a Corporation bus from that of other operators (such as Ribble, Lancashire United, Bolton Corporation etc.) which used similar looking buses and had a similar looking livery at first glance. The choice of green marker lights is probably due to the fact that green or white were permissable colours at the front of a vehicle, whereas red was not. Lancashire United buses carried three small white marker lights, usually placed below the indicator panel, for a similar reason. In tramway days, some towns used coloured lights to indicate route, whilst others used a green marker light at the front as a signal to an approaching tram that the car showing green was waiting in a loop and was not blocking the line.

Vehicle Design

Much conservatism was shown in choosing the design of the vehicles, as after the major purchase of Leyland Titan TD1 buses to replace the trams, the same type of timber framed body was specified for orders fulfilled in 1932, 1933, 1936, 1937 and 1938. The same applies to single deckers of 1932, 1933 and 1936. Even metal-framed bus bodies of 1939-40, of modern appearance, retained a low capacity of 48 seats which were arranged 24 on the lower deck and 24 on the upper deck. Upstairs the bench seats for four were interspersed with benches for three, giving improved circulation. Post war vehicles with Leyland bodies followed the normal national pattern, but Wigan shunned rear engined double deck designs for some time, preferring to keep to front-engined half-cab buses. Wigan also reverted to exposed radiator types

Double deckers & low bridges

Before discussing the evolution of the Wigan double deck bus, it must be made clear that Wigan, and surrounding towns like Leigh and St. Helens, were full of low level bridges, mostly railway bridges. All the standard gauge trams originally purchased for use in Wigan were single deckers, as were all buses bought before 1929. Six double deck top-covered trams were placed in service in Wigan in 1914, with 18 more entering service in 1920-22, but these cars were restricted in their movements.

Until pneumatic tyres and cranked (low-loading) chassis were introduced for use on buses in the twenties, double deckers with top covers were about sixteen feet high. In 1927, Leyland Motors developed a revolutionary new model, influenced by American practice, which had a low-loading chassis and a "stepped" body. The bus and its body were named "Titan" by Leyland, but the style of the body, which at about thirteen feet six inches was able to pass under all but extremely constricted road over-bridges, came to be known as "lowbridge" (The corresponding slightly higher body with a flat upper deck floor became known as "highbridge", and these terms will appear further in this book.)

The picture above shows the upper deck of a Leyland-bodied Leyland Titan bus of the 1946-50 period, and is similar to the 75 buses purchased by Wigan Corporation just before and just after the Second World War. The bus has 53 seats (27 on the upper deck) and a low gangway on the offside which gives access to the seats and allows the conductor to collect the fares. In pre-war days, Wigan specified a lesser number of seats on the upper deck by having shorter benches for three alternating with the bench seats for four. (Photograph by Ron Phillips)

The First Leylands

In early 1927, the Corporation were requiring new buses. Thornycroft gave a demonstration in January, and were favoured with an order for 6 chassis - the bodies being built locally, 2 each from the local coachbuilders (Massey, NCME, Santus). In March, consideration was given to the replacement of trams on the Platt Bridge route, and Bristol gave a demonstration of its latest low-loading bus - the result, an order for six chassis with NCME bodies. A seventh example was ordered in August (and was shown at the Olympia Motor Show) and two more were ordered in October, this time with Bristol bodies, to speed delivery. Leyland were able to secure an order at the same time by quoting 14 day delivery on two Lions....these arrived in November.

When more new buses were needed in 1928, the Committee met in February and inspected several demonstration buses and purchased a Pagefield, a Bristol B and another Leyland Lion. Two more of the locally made Pagefield chassis were ordered at the same time, and three more Bristols were ordered later. But this was to be the end of a rather haphazard vehicle ordering policy.

Wigan had purchased its first Leylands, three of the best-selling PLSC1 Lion type, in November 1927, EK 6042-6043, fleet numbers 9 and 10. and in March 1928, EK 6281 fleet number 7. They joined a fleet entirely made up of single deckers of Bristol, Pagefield, Karrier and Thornycroft manufacture.

They clearly gave the right impression, and the Transport Committee agreed to buy nothing but Leylands after 1930. When discussing the purchase of new vehicles with the Transport Committee, the General Manager would obtain the price of Leyland chassis before the meeting, and only the tenders for bodywork would be discussed, it being taken as read that the make of chassis would be Leyland. The reasons behind this policy to buy chassis from only one manufacturer were standardisation and efficiency, things which the previous fleet of many makes and styles had not been able to give.

The trio of PLSC Lions survived in revenue service until 1939, by which time they were the longest-serving buses ever owned by Wigan up to that date. When they were overhauled in November 1937, they were praised for their longevity (each was said to have covered 400,000 miles) and were all given Certificates of Fitness valid until December 1940. They became surplus in 1938 when three modern LT9 Lions were delivered, but remained in stock until early 1939 when they were given, free of charge, for use by the local A.R.P. (Air Raid Precautions).

A photograph of these three buses appears on pages 24-25. The specially posed view was arranged by Leyland Motors at the time when Wigan Corporation was about to decide to replace the tramway system with a fleet of 48 seat lowbridge Leyland Titan TD1 buses. The seven double deckers seen in the picture were already in service, and had given such satisfaction in regard to mechanical reliability and economy of operation in comparison with the time expired tramcars and the mixed fleet of motor buses then in use, that without hesitation it was agreed to scrap the tramways at the earliest possible date and substitute them with Leyland buses.

The First Leyland Titans

At a meeting of the Transport Committee on 23rd September 1929 it was agreed that four double deck Leyland Titans be ordered. Terms had clearly been discussed in advance with Leyland, as it was disclosed that Leyland would accept in part exchange four 20 seat Thornycrofts. The price for the four new vehicles would be £6100, which gave the "usual discount" and £125 each for the Thornycrofts. The money was to be paid from the Transport Department's reserve fund. The reason for purchasing the 48 seat double deckers was to replace the seven 20-seat vehicles then employed on the Platt Bridge service. The Leyland offer to purchase four of these was in line with the company's policy at the time (one vehicle per vehicle ordered) and the little buses passed directly to Tillotson (dealer) at Burnley. The new Titan buses, delivered in November 1929, were EK 7260-3 and took numbers 2, 4, 5, 6. The Thornycrofts sold were 2 , 3, 4, 6. At the same time, ominously, the Committee sanctioned the scrapping of eight disused tramcars. In effect the first tram route had been replaced by Titans.

So successful was the introduction of the Titans that at the Committee Meeting in December it was decided to buy three more for the Beech Hill route. Again three 20 seat Thornycrofts (1,11,13) were to be traded in at £125 each and £4,575 would be borrowed to pay for the double deckers. They entered service in March 1930. with the registrations EK 7434-6, and fleet numbers 1, 3, 11 (the "unlucky" number 13 would not be re-used until 1946.)

The first Leyland Titan TD1 buses for Wigan Corporation Tramways were built in October 1929. Here is No.2 (EK 7260) seen before delivery. The earliest enclosed back Leyland bodies had a fixed upper deck window, as seen here.   (BCVMA)

These pictures show Titans at work on the Beech Hill service, taken at the same time as the cover picture. The first Titans did not display route numbers. Above is a bus under one of Wigan's many overbridges....the track in the street is a colliery railway. Below is a picture taken in Mesnes Road, showing that not all of Wigan was like the rather bleak scene above. There is a lot of pleasant countryside around the town, and in the thirties the Corporation ran Sunday afternoon tours !   (BCVMA)

Replacing the Trams

By the spring of 1930 the Wigan tramways were becoming run down. There had been no discussion of replacing them as a whole, but the issue was brought into focus by the success of the new Titan buses and an ultimatum from Ashton in Makerfield to discontinue the arrangements for the use of the tram tracks within that urban district. Wigan negotiated a "stay of execution" for the Ashton line until 30th November 1930, and agreed to substitute the trams by motor buses or trackless vehicles.

A debate followed over the summer; in the end the trackless option was dropped and in August 1930 a decision was taken to replace all the tram services with 38 new double deck buses. Because of the deadline set with Ashton in Makerfiled, at least nine buses were needed by November. Tenders were invited for complete vehicles or for chassis and bodies separately, with final delivery required by March 1931.

On 2nd September 1930 a special meeting of the Tramways Committee was held, with Messrs. Windsor and Allen of Leyland Motors present A provisional agreement was reached with Leyland to supply nine or ten complete double deckers by the end of November, and twenty further Titan chassis for supply to local coachbuilders, who would mount bodies to a design which would not infringe the patent rights held by Leyland. The price agreed was £1650 per complete vehicle and £949 per chassis.

Two days later, another special meeting was held with Mr.Fone of N.C.M.E., Mr. I. Massey and Messrs.Santus (Snr. & Jnr.) representing the three Wigan bus bodybuilding firms. The outcome was a provisional agreement that the three firms would build double deck bodies to the Leyland design at £700 per body: Santus would construct two, and the others ten each.

This had now to be settled with Leyland. A high-level meeting was arranged at Wigan on 17th September 1930, attended by Mr.Liardet, General Manager of Leyland Motors. The Transport Department minutes report:

'Leyland Motors were prepared to make a special concession in the case of the vehicles to be built for the Corporation by allowing the local bodybuilders to copy the "Titan" design on payment of £1 instead of the usual charge of £50.

'Mr. Liardet said the concession was a special one made on this occasion only and for the benefit of the Corporation, owing to the relations existing between their firm and the Corporation as regards the employment of Wigan labour.

'Mr. Liardet referred to the suggestion of the Tramways' Manager that an emergency door should be constructed in the off-side of the lower saloon in complete vehicles to be supplied by Leyland Motors, and offered (on behalf of his firm) to supply such emergency door for an additional sum of £14 per vehicle. He added, however, that if the Corporation would be prepared to increase the number of complete omnibuses which they were prepared to obtain direct from Leyland Motors from ten to fifteen, his company would undertake to supply vehicles with emergency doors as before-mentioned for the sum originally quoted, namely £1650.'

And so a deal was done, and Wigan got all its new buses at £1650 each ! The final arrangement for 38 buses was as follows:

1. Leyland were to supply nine (not ten) complete vehicles in time for the closure of the Ashton tram service. These were EK 7906-14, Nos.38-46, delivered for December 1st 1930, when they entered service.

2. Leyland were to supply an additional six complete vehicles, bringing their part of the order to fifteen, during March 1931. These were EK 8039-44, Nos.47-52.

3. Leyland were to supply 23 chassis to the Wigan coachbuilders. N.C.M.E. would body 10, Massey would body 10 (as previously agreed), and Santus would body 3. (The Santus allocation was increased by one by subsequent agreement).

The 23 vehicles were as follows:

53-54	EK 8086-87	N.C.M.E.
55-56	EK 8088-89	Massey
57-59	EK 8090-91, EK 8116	Santus
60-67	EK 8100-7	N.C.M.E.
68-75	EK 8108-15	Massey

All the buses were built to the Leyland drawings, and entered service during March and April 1931. The last trams ran on 28th March 1931, with the official last car and official first bus running on the Abbey Lakes Route.

The 38 tram replacement buses differed from the 7 previous Titan TD1s in having route number boxes mounted on the front, above the standard Titan indicator. The blind for this number box was turned by a handle inside the upper saloon; although not a standard fitting, these number boxes were an extra supplied by Leyland to customers who needed to show route numbers. They also had the above-mentioned emergency door, installed in the first off-side bay of the lower saloon. This was not a statutory requirement, and in the case of Wigan was the result of a rule instigated by the Chief Constable. The seven existing Titans, seen on pages 24-25, were fitted with route number boxes in 1931, and with opening rear emergency windows subsequently. Apart from the next four (trolleybus replacement) double deckers, the lower deck emergency exit was not perpetuated in Wigan, as new Construction and Use Regulations, introduced by the Road Traffic Act (1930), overrode local regulations.

The form of application of the livery on the Titans set the pattern for many years to come. The first seven TD1s carried the legend "Wigan Corporation Tramways", as seen on the front cover, but this was then reduced to "Wigan Corporation". The town's coat of arms was applied centrally onto the upper and lower deck side panels, and the fleet numbers were displayed centrally on the lower rear panel and twice at the front on half-cab buses, below the windscreen and on the bulkhead. Pre-war buses which had "autovacs" (a small tank attached to the front bulkhead from which fuel was fed to the engine) had the fleet number applied to the autovac, which was painted white. When the full width bonnets on models PD2/20, PD3/2 etc. were introduced, the fleet numbers appeared twice on the front, but flat-fronted designs showed one centrally placed number. Even after the simplification of the livery (see rear cover, lower picture) the livery remained distinctive. It in fact survives today on trucks and vans in service with the Metropolitan Borough Council of Wigan.

The Trolleybuses go too

The Martland Mill tram service, the last to run on the narrow gauge, was closed to trams on 7th May 1925, the route then being taken over by trolleybuses later that same day. The cars were broken up at the depot in Woodhouse Lane and the building was demolished. The Watch Committee would not allow the trolleybuses to turn at the Market Place, so they terminated at the foot of Market Street.

Four vehicles were obtained to run the service. Numbered 1-4, (EK 3967-70) they had Straker-Clough chassis, built at Edmonton, BTH electrical equipment, and Brush centre-entrance 37 seat single deck bodies.Complaints of vibration from house-holders in Woodhouse Lane instigated the fitting of pneumatic tyres on the front axles by mid 1928. They were last overhauled in July-August 1930, by which time pneumatic tyres had been fitted to the rear axles also.

In March 1930, Guy Motors asked if they could demonstrate their latest type of trolleybus, free of charge. This was agreed to, and on 31st March 1930 a 60 seat double deck Guy trolleybus made several demonstration runs on the Martland Mill route in the presence of a civic delegation. However, although the trolleybuses had been satisfactory and were considered as a possible replacement for broad gauge tram routes, the need to promote a Parliamentary Act proved a stumbling block.

Having replaced the last tram services in March 1931, the Corporation found itself with a "White Elephant", as the Martland Mill route was once again isolated as it had been when it was the only narrow gauge tram route. The trackless cars had to travel to and from the depot each day over the now disused tram tracks which had to be left exposed in the roadway to allow trolleybuses to trail a skate for the return current.

The General Manager delivered a report to the Committee on 18th May 1931. In it he argued that replacement of the trolley buses by petrol driven buses would be of financial benefit. It would cost £250 to alter the existing overhead between the Market Place and the Central Depot to allow for the filling in of the tram tracks and it was necessary to retain the tower wagon and a line crew for overhead maintenance. If buses took over, neither of the former would be necessary and the route could be joined with the New Springs service.

The Committee accepted the Manager's recommendations, and instructed that application be made to the Traffic Commissioners for a road service licence and that Leyland should be asked to tender for four vehicles for prompt delivery. An order was placed in June for 4 Titans with Leyland bodywork at £1606 each. This price is £44 less than was paid earlier in the year, but in November 1930 the Corporation had made an agreement with the Michelin Tyre Company to lease tyres on a mileage basis and the price shown probably excludes tyres. The new vehicles were EK 8330-3, Nos.76-9 and entered service on 1st October 1930. The four trolleybuses were sold to a scrap merchant along with the overhead equipment.

Wigan Corporation now had 49 lowbridge Leyland Titans and a variety of older single deck buses in a fleet of 78 units. All were driven by petrol engines.

Diesel versus Petrol

In the local parlance of the people of Wigan and the surrounding district in the nineteen-thirties, motor buses were "petrol buses". This term arose in order to make the distinction between trolley buses, introduced in Wigan in 1925 and on the South Lancs Tramways, serving Ashton, Platt Bridge, Hindley, Leigh and Bolton from 1930. At first, of course, it was quite correct, but during 1931-1932, bus manufacturers introduced compression-ignition engines, known at the time as "oil-engines" and today as "diesel-engines."

The new engines were more expensive to buy, heavier and noisier than petrol engines, and more likely to cause vibrations. But they were cheaper to run, as will be explained on page 18. Wigan took one of the first Leyland made diesel engines in bus number 83 of 1932. The engine was so new that the manufacturer arranged to keep an eye on its performance during the first twelve months. Wigan was satisfied, and when next ordering buses in 1933 specified oil engines. Four of the new buses were single deckers, so the engines were exchanged with the petrol units in the newest Titan TD1 buses, numbers 76-79. Following this a programme of replacing petrol engines in all Wigan buses was started, but came to an end when there were only 24 double deckers still driven by petrol. It was obviously felt that the life left in these buses would not justify the expense of buying new engines.

On the left can be seen the only Wigan bus not to have carried a Wigan registration number, No.12, HO 6387, was a Thornycroft demonstrator. The scene is Market St. and the wires are those to allow the trolleybuses to return to the depot.   (BCVMA)

TD2s and Tigers

The year 1932 was to be free of the numerous worries and financial problems which had beset the town's tramways. There was, however, a new problem to keep the Transport Committee busy. (The Tramways Committee had been renamed Transport Committee on 25th August 1931) The Road Traffic Act, 1930, had introduced road service licencing, and Wigan was served by a multitude of bus routes. There was a constant need to protect the Transport Department's interests with every road service licence application.

In March 1932 the General Manager announced that he intended to purchase 13 new buses to cope with increasing traffic and to dispose of old single-deck buses which were costly to operate. Ten of the new buses would be double-deckers and one would be powered by an oil engine. Tenders were called for and received.

There followed a series of back-stage manoeuvres involving Mr. Liardet and other Leyland managers, and on 23rd May 1932 the Committee met and was informed that Leyland Motors could supply chassis at the following prices:

Double-deck chassis (petrol engine) at £845
Double-deck chassis (oil engine) at £1020
Single-deck chassis (petrol engine) at £830

The Committee then toured the three local bodybuilder's offices to discuss terms for bodies to be put on the chassis, and made the following decision to order.

9 Titan petrol engined chassis to be fitted with N.C.M.E. bodies at £601 each
3 Tiger petrol engined chassis to be fitted with Santus bodies at £390 each
1 Titan oil engined chassis with Leyland body at £1665 for the complete vehicle.

There is no mention in the minutes of a royalty to be paid by N.C.M.E. to build a body to the lowbridge design, but the quoted price of £601 suggests that a nominal £1 fee was paid. The Santus single deck bodies were also built to Leyland design, but this was not subject to a patent fee. No deal was struck regarding the vehicles to be replaced, but Leyland was to monitor the oil engined bus for a period.

The money to pay for these vehicles was to be borrowed, and to secure the loan it was necessary to tell the Ministry of Transport to what purpose they were being put, that is, replacements. Public money could not be spent on speculative purchases at a time when there was fierce competition in the Traffic Courts as operators sought to define and defend their territories. The nine single deckers to be replaced were offered for sale by tender. Three Bristols went to St.Helens Corporation, three Pagefields to Granville Tours, Grimsby and of three Karriers, one went to an owner in Cumberland and two were disposed of locally.

The new petrol engined double deckers (of type TD2) took the numbers of the withdrawn vehicles 21, 23, 27-30, 32-4 (EK 8859-77), but the Tigers (type TS4) and the oil-engined Titan were 80-3 (EK 8866-8, 8878). All these new buses entered service in October 1932. As far as the general public were concerned, the new TD2 double deckers were the same in appearance as the previous TD1s.

The TD2 chassis was an improvement in many ways over the TD1, and it is interesting to see how Wigan at this period was happy to include the latest innovations on the chassis of its buses, but remained extremely conservative with regard to the bodywork. One would have thought that having got rid of the tramcars, whose history had been troublesome to say the least, the Corporation would have tried to have shown a "modern" face to the public.

The illustration above shows the style of single deck bus chosen by Wigan, it is Tiger TS4 No.18 (EK 9312) of 1933, with bodywork by Massey Brothers. Like many municipal single deckers, the doorway to the 32 seat body is at the rear. Passengers living in a town where rear platform double deckers predominated, would naturally move towards the back of a bus as it drew up at the kerbside. Some towns, Edinburgh for instance, even fitted a wide inset entrance at the rear to be more like the open doorway of a double decker, but Wigan specified a narrow entrance with a folding door as seen here. Note the two green lights flanking the route indicator. On pre-war Wigan single deckers, the route number was displayed in a separate box which can just be discerened in the picture under the canopy.

Wigan was slightly unusual in choosing the Leyland Tiger, with six cylinder engine, for its single deck fleet. In general, municipal operators chose the four cylinder engined Lion model, but as will be seen, when Wigan did buy some Lions with the less powerful engine, within six months six cylinder units were installed. The reason for the change was probably a mixture of driver preference, a desire for standardisation, and (perhaps), a preference for a less noisy engine. Although Wigan chose to fit diesel engines to most of the fleet after 1932, there were still petrol engined buses at work in the town until 1945, and although these were more expensive to operate, the Leyland six cylinder petrol engines were renowned for their smoothness and quietness. The pre-war diesel engines were quite noisy compared with the Leyland petrol engines, and it was their cheap fuel which was their main attraction.

15

An all-Leyland Fleet

After the purchases of 1932, there remained just 14 buses in the fleet of 82 which were not of Leyland Motors' manufacture. At the Transport Committee meeting of February 1933 it was explained that an order for 14 new vehicles was needed, to replace old single deck vehicles. Leyland Motors had quoted a price of £1025 each for oil-engined chassis, and once again the committee members adjourned to visit the premises of the local coachbuilders. It was subsequently agreed that NCME would supply ten double deck bodies (to the existing design based on the Leyland lowbridge body) at £575 per bus. Single deck bodies would be supplied by Massey (3) and Santus (1). It should be noted that although the fleet was not being expanded, ten of the new buses were double deckers with a larger seating capacity than the single deckers being withdrawn.

The new buses took the numbers of the vehicles they replaced, and it is possible that there was some form of arrangement with Leyland over the disposal of these vehicles. The double deckers on Titan TD2 chassis were numbered 19-20, 22,24-26, 31, 35-37 (EK 9313-22); the single deckers on Tiger TS4 chassis were 8 (EK 9309) with Santus body and 16-18 (EK 9310-12) with Massey bodies. Delivery of the latter was late, and the Corporation complained that it had been necessary to relicense three vehicles they had expected to withdraw on June 1st. A court case ensued.

The goal of an all-Leyland fleet was almost won, but attention now turned to reducing the number of petrol-engined vehicles. In December 1933 the Manager presented the argument for fitting new oil engines (at a cost of £490 per bus) into 14 existing double deckers. Because of the differential between the price of petrol and that of diesel fuel, the expense would be recouped in 16 months. The order was placed and the new engines were installed by Leyland Motors at their Chorley Works by March 1934. In August 11 more engines were ordered on the same terms, and in February 1935 12 more engines (this time less dynamos) were ordered at £455. After these had been installed, the fleet contained 52 oil-engined vehicles and 30 petrol-engined.

In the Budget of April 1935 it was announced that the tax on diesel fuel was to be increased (implemented August 1935) so that the incentive to re-engine more older buses was reduced, and no further conversions were made. The increase in tax was heavy, seven pence per gallon, but this increase was partly offset by reductions in the fees of Road Fund licences.

Three new vehicles were ordered in September 1935 to replace the last three Thornycrofts, and thereby create an all-Leyland fleet. These were to be two Leyland Titan TD4 and one Tiger TS7. They were the first examples of the improved Leyland range in the Corporation fleet, but the timber-framed bodies retained the styling of the earlier Leylands. NCME built the double deckers, Nos.12 and 14 (JP 1211-12) and Santus the 32 seat rear-entrance body on No.15 (JP 1213). The old Thornycrofts were sold by the Corporation to a dealer, with the stipulation that they were not to be used as dwellings within the borough !

The single deckers of 1932, 1933 and 1936 like their double deck counterparts had timber-framed bodies to a similar and rather archaic design, based on the Leyland single deck bodies of the 1930 period. One particular feature was the shallow arched tops to the side windows. This old fashioned bodywork sat badly on the Tiger TS7 chassis of No.15 (JP 1213). In the picture above it is seen after "modernisation" in its old age........it was converted into a mobile library for Leigh Corporation.

The first diesel engined bus in the Wigan fleet, No.83 (EK 8878) of 1932, is seen when new at the Leyland Works. Note the unusual position of the rear registration number, and the transfer on the off-side for Dewandre brakes, usually associated with the Ribble fleet.   (BCVMA)

17

Fleet Expansion

The General Manager told his Committee in July 1936 that he required ten new double deck buses "to augment and maintain the high standard and efficiency of the fleet of omnibuses", and that Leyland should be approached for the supply of the chassis and the local coachbuilders for the supply of bodywork. Three of the new buses were wanted as soon as possible, and the rest by the end of the financial year (i.e. 31st March 1937). They would be paid for out of revenue.

Leyland quoted £837 each for Titan TD4 chassis: Massey and NCME quoted £685 each for bodywork to the "piano-fronted" design. Each coachbuilder received an order for five bodies, with Massey to supply the first three as soon as possible. When these three were being built, it was decided to increase the order by two more buses, with an extra body from each coachbuilder. As all of these were additional buses, they were numbered 84-95. Such was the good financial state of the transport department at this time, that not only were the new buses paid for out of revenue, but bus fares were reduced from 1st April 1937. The twelve new buses were delivered as follows:

84-86	JP 1925-27	Massey bodies, licensed in 12/36
87-93	JP 2025-31	Massey & NCME, licensed in 3/37
94-95	JP 2195-96	Massey & NCME, licensed in 5/37 & 4/37

There is some confusion over which buses had Massey bodies and which had NCME, but the first three are known to have been built by Massey.

The crowded scene at the Market Place in 1947, when the motor bus remained the principal form of transport. Leyland TD4 No.89 (JP 2027) of 1937 is seen on route 9 to Pemberton. The Massey bodywork (timber-framed) is built to the Leyland design of 1929 and was somewhat out of date. (BCVMA)

The First Leylands Replaced

In March 1938 the Transport Committee met to consider the purchase of new buses, intended to be the first in a cycle of replacement for the existing fleet. For the first time, the General Manager considered ordering all-metal bodywork, and produced a list of six coachbuilding firms offering this type of construction. This meant the abandonment of the "old-fashioned" look for the Wigan buses, and to an extent the abandonment of the policy to obtain bus bodies from local firms. However, the choice of Leyland for the chassis was not open to debate

Eighteen vehicles were to be purchased, three single deckers to replace the three 1927-8 Lions, and fifteen double deckers to replace an equal quantity of early Titan TD1s. All were to have diesel engines and all-metal bodies. The tenders for the bodywork were opened in May, and the orders were duly placed as follows:

3 Leyland Lion LT9 chassis with 4 cylinder diesel engines (at £850 each)
    3 rear entrance 32 seat bodies by Northern Counties (at £604 each)
15 Leyland Titan TD5 diesel engined chassis (at £1015 each)
    10 Leyland metal-framed 48 seat bodies (at £875 each)
    3   English Electric metal-framed 48 seat bodies (at £850 each)
    2   Northern Counties metal-framed 48 seat bodies (at £871 each)

The three single deckers came in December, as replacements for the old Lions which were still in good working order. The new LT9s took numbers 104-6 and not 7, 9 and 10 as carried by the obsolete buses which remained in service until March 1939. After this they continued in civic ownership to act in a civil defence role, and new double deckers took their fleet numbers (see below). The four-cylinder engines fitted to the LT9s clearly did not give satisfaction, and whilst still less than 6 months old, 104-106 were returned to Leyland's Chorley Works for six-cylinder engines to be fitted. This work was undertaken at a specially agreed price of £100 per vehicle.

The fifteen double deckers arrived in March-April 1939. The three with English Electric bodies took the numbers 7, 9, 10 vacated by the PLSC Lions, but the remainder took the numbers to new heights, those with NCME bodies were 107-8, and the ten all-Leyland buses were allocated 109-119, with the number 113 (like 13) being avoided. It is clear that the growing traffic caused by the increased economic activity in the build up to World War Two, made the disposal of the oldest Titans impossible, and 10 were retained in service, 4 were stored and one converted to a service vehicle. The fleet in mid 1939 stood at 112 operational buses, all Leylands, (with 4 in store making 116), and fleet numbers from 1-119 (13, 65 and 113 not being used).

Leyland LT9s

It is interesting to record here a fact relating to the three Lion LT9s. In 1949 the Corporation ordered replacement chassis frames from Leyland to fit to these buses, at a cost of £50 per frame. Such renewal is unusual, although not unique. The vehicles continued in service until 1954-6, when they were replaced by Tiger Cubs. One, No.104, then went to South Africa for use on missionary work !

Leyland Fleet Series - Wigan Corporation

The chassis of the LT9 was to the same dimensions at the contemporary Tiger, as can be seen in the illustration on this page, and at first glance the bus looks like a Tiger TS7 or TS8. Once fitted with six cylinder engines, Nos.104-106 were Tigers in all but name.

Leyland LT9 single decker with all-metal N.C.M.E. body is waiting to enter service outside the Central Depot. Note the white painted autovac carrying the fleet number, and the route number box placed above, partly blocking the bulkhead window.

(photo courtesy H.Wall)

Leyland LT9 No.105 is standing at the Market Place in front of the Transport Offices. This point was the hub of operations in both the tramway and motor bus era.

(photo courtesy H.Wall)

The Onset of War

1939 was a good year for Wigan buses. Page 19 told how the delivery of fifteen new double deckers did not lead to the disposal of a similar number of older vehicles, and brought the fleet to 116. In September, the month when war was declared, the Transport Committee met and decided to order 14 double deckers to replace the 14 Titans due for replacement earlier in the year, but which had been given a reprieve. This decision was formalised in October when an order was placed with Leyland for 14 Titan TD7 chassis with Leyland metal-framed lowbridge bodies. Prices, at £1008 for a chassis and £897 for a body, showed only a slight variation from the prices of the buses delivered a few months earlier.

In March 1940, Leyland wrote to advise of a price increase. Despite this, the Committee felt it was time to order more new vehicles, and told Leyland that they would require 14 more similar buses in May 1940, increasing this request to 28 in June. As things turned out, only the 1939 order was fully completed, the new buses arriving in June-July, and allowing 10 of the older TD1s to be hired to Leigh, who were desperate for vehicles to transport war workers. Of the further 28, only 3 were to come in 1942. The 1940 delivery (JP 4700-13) took the numbers of the petrol-engined TD1s 2, 4-6, 60-4, 66-8 and 70-1 which now formed a "reserve fleet"(see overleaf) and had another five years of Wigan ownership ahead of them.

Leyland TD7 No.60 of 1940 shows up the fine detail of the Wigan Corporation livery. (Note the TD7 model does not have the bulkhead mounted autovac of earlier Titan models.) When in service, the tyres would be further embellished with white walls. The body is an all-metal 48 seater by Leyland.   (BCVMA)

The Wartime Period 1940-45

In the summer of 1940 the total of buses owned by Wigan Corporation rose to 116 plus 14. The Titan TD1s intended to be disposed of remained on the books, with a small plain black letter "A" alongside the shaded gold fleet numerals , thus 64 . It had not been proposed to keep these buses, and indeed the Leyland Western Sales Manager had reported their intended fate in a memo of February 1940:

'Second hand double deck buses are in demand, the prices having risen from roundabout £25 per machine pre-war to anything up to £100. Many municipalities are refusing to sell off their old machines and are prepared to hire out to other Bodies any redundant or, for the moment, overplus stock.

'Another example of what is being done is Wigan Corporation's intentions when the 14 new double deck buses due next month are delivered, to break up the old double deckers they replace and keep all the spare parts, stocks of aluminium panels, pumps, window panes and frames for replacement parts on other buses'

In fact the 14 buses escaped the rather bizarre fate of being broken down into sets of parts by their owner, as they were a more useful asset in one piece. The LPTB in London had set a precedent early in the war, hiring provincial buses to cover those vehicles damaged in air raids at £25 per month, and this became the standard price of bus hire (the same for double or single deckers) throughout the wartime period. Thus

Bus number 65 (EK 8105) was converted into this smart looking breakdown tender in 1939 by the Corporation. The white-wall tyres are an unusual feature. (BCVMA)

the 13 buses hired to Leigh Corporation from June, 10 TD1s and 3 single deck TS4s, were worth almost £4000 per annum in revenue. Along with the hired buses went two TIM ticket machines, the only ones then owned by Wigan. Leigh obtained more of these machines from Southend. Wigan continued with punch type tickets until 1948, when the TIM system was adopted.

The hired buses were used to serve a huge munitions factory which was being constructed at Risley, which lay on the Leigh to Warrington route, and lowbridge machines were essential. The ten surplus TD1s of the "reserve fleet" sent to Leigh are believed to have been 2A, 4A, 6A, 63A, 64A, 66-68A and 70-71A, along with three single deck Tigers, Nos.80-2. Four TD1s remained in store: Nos. 5A, 60-2A. Circumstances at Leigh changed in the later part of the War. In mid 1941 there were 21 hired vehicles in a fleet of nearly 80 (doubling the 1939 total), but by late 1943 Leigh was itself offering some of its older petrol-engined buses for hire.

Producer Gas Buses

Late in 1942 bus operators were told that in view of the fuel shortage, they should arrange to convert up to 10% of their fleet to operate on "producer gas". This gas was generated by a small furnace the size of an oil drum which was towed behind the bus on a two-wheeled trailer . The system was only applicable on petrol engined vehicles and engine power was very limited, causing problems for operators with hilly terrain. Bus operators were expected to have the gas buses on the road by July 1943. The Wigan engineer was sent to see the system in operation at Grays (with the LPTB) and Maldon (with the Eastern National Omnibus Company), and the necessary equipment was ordered. Like most towns, Wigan did not relish the idea of producer gas buses and delayed converting any until the last minute. Eventually gas buses were used on the Martland Mill - New Springs service, said to be the least hilly. The exact date of commencement is not clear, but was probably July 1943 starting with one vehicle. Buses known to have operated with producer gas are 1, 2A, 5A, 62A and 67A, all petrol-engined TD1s. There may have been a sixth, but the proposed total of 12 was never reached. What is clearly stated is that the last day of gas bus operation was Saturday 16th September 1944.

The Wartime Buses

The demands of the war effort were such that the Ministry of War Transport froze all bus production, and then allowed the vehicle manufacturers to finish off any buses which were partly built or for which the component parts had been made. The operators had to put in an application for a "Licence to Acquire", and the MoWT was responsible for the distribution of the few vehicles available to the most needy of the operators. Of the 28 Leylands on order, Wigan Corporation was to receive just three.

In April 1942 Leyland Motors informed Wigan that two TD7s with Leyland bodies were allocated, and the cost would be £2224 per vehicle (an increase of over £300 compared with the 1940 delivery.) When these arrived, they were found to be fitted with lowbridge bodies intended for Alexander: there was no rear destination blind, and the front destination and number box were surmounted by an illuminated panel (which was not used at Wigan, of course). These were the first Wigan buses to

A specially posed publicity shot taken in March 1930 shows the ten Leylands then in service.
seven Titans helped to persuade the Committee that the motor bus was the best alternative to
afterwards to replace the trolleybuses. The vehicles depicted are Lions 10, 9 and 7, and Titan
1929 with an enamelled "Titan" head, but this type of radiator seems to have been unsatisfac

have three-track number boxes and moquette (rather than leather) covered seats. They took fleet numbers 120-121 (JP 4816-7).

The third vehicle was another TD7, but this time fitted with an East Lancs body. Delivered in August 1942, it became 122 (JP 4922), and like the other pair had 53 seats (the then normal capacity for this type of bus), rather than the more spacious allocation of 48 seats as used hitherto in Wigan. One advantage of the lower capacity was greater circulation room for both passengers and conductors, however.

Bus number 63, one of the 1940 delivery of TD7s, was destroyed by fire at Aspull on Sunday 22nd August 1943. The General Manager got in touch with the Regional Transport Commissioner, and arrangements were made via official channels for Leyland to repair the vehicle. Leyland at that point in time had no bodybuilding facilities, and arranged with Alexanders at Falkirk to reconstruct a body to Leyland specification. The Alexander bodyworks had completed some Leyland metal-framed bodies in 1942 and were engaged in building new double deck bodies which were very similar to the Leyland design for various Scottish bus fleets. In April 1944, however, the Corporation was told that Alexanders were not able to build the body,

:ture was taken at a time when the future of the tramways was uncertain. The success of the
's, and 38 Titans were subsequently ordered to replace trams, with a further 4 ordered shortly
5, 4, 3, 2 and 1. Numbers 6 and 5 have the radiator fitted when they were new in November
1 numbers 4 and 2 have already had them replaced.   (BCVMA)

and that the order would be fulfilled by Northern Coach Builders of Newcastle.

No.63 duly returned to service in 1944. The fleet now stood at 133 buses, made up of 119 plus the reserve of 14. As early as December 1942 Wigan Corporation were in touch with Leyland's Western Sales Manager in Manchester to reserve buses for delivery as soon as peace-time conditions returned. It was suggested that the existing order for 25 (the residue of the 28 ordered in 1940) should be increased to 50, but it was then decided that 75 buses should be reserved, and a formal letter of intent to purchase was sent to Leyland Motors. These buses were delivered in 1946-7 as told on the next page, but before this Wigan took delivery of the six utility buses.

The Utility Buses

There was no sign of Leyland Motors resuming bus chassis production in early 1944, and some of the older Titans were in urgent need of replacement. Consequently the Ministry of War Transport granted a licence for Wigan to receive three utility buses, on Bristol K6A chassis powered by AEC 7.7 litre oil engines, and with low bridge bodywork by Strachans. The letter of the MoWT arrived on the 8th May, and the General Manager somewhat reluctantly wrote " as the licence would cease to have effect unless the order was placed within a month, I have in the circumstances issued orders in accordance with the MoWT's directions." Despite the seeming urgency, the three vehicles were not delivered until one year later, in May 1945.

Although Leyland had not yet resumed production of vehicles for civilian use, the Company was being allowed to re-condition engines from older vehicles and to build a few new engines for sale to transport firms. Wigan was allowed to purchase four 8.6 litre engines "to be used solely for replacement purposes, but not to be used as permanent replacements." It is not clear how Wigan employed these units. The intention was to allow a 'float' of engines to permit older units to be reconditioned without the bus they belonged to being put out of service. In August 1944, the MoWT once more issued a licence to acquire three more lowbridge utility buses, this time on Guy Arab chassis with Gardner 5LW engines and Weymann bodies. They arrived seven months later in March 1945, taking fleet numbers 123-125 (JP 5130-32) and were followed by the Bristols in May and June, as Nos.126-8 (JP 5133-5). 124 arrived in an all-over grey livery, in which it ran for a while. All the utility buses except 128 had wooden seats when new, although these were later replaced. Other features of these angular looking buses were wooden frames, steel panels, and poor ventilation. Also, they did not have the two green marker lights at the front.

In view of the non-standard nature of these utility buses in an otherwise all-Leyland fleet, they had quite short lives at Wigan and were never rebuilt to a better specification as happened in many towns. The Guys were withdrawn in 1951 and the Bristols lasted a little longer until 1956-8. Wigan were also offered Crossley chassis, but managed to avoid purchasing yet another non standard type.

The Leyland body on this TD7 (No.121) was assembled from parts intended for the Scottish Bus Group, but released to Wigan in 1942. Note the restricted ventilation, with no opening windows on the offside of the upper deck.　　(H. Wall collection)

One odd fact about the wartime Wigan fleet is that it was dependent upon the Titans scheduled for withdrawal in 1939, reprieved until 1940, hired in 1940 to Leigh Corporation, and taken back into service in Wigan from 1943 when Leigh had taken in a fleet of utility style Guy Arabs. These TD1s were disposed of after the war along with the rest of the 1929-1931 deliveries, and many were to be sold for further service, either directly by Wigan Corporation, or via dealers (see page 30).

The only Titan actually withdrawn in 1939 was No.65 (EK 8105), which became the breakdown wagon. It remained in use until 1953, when it was replaced by another wagon based on a bus chassis. This was ex-No.102 (JP 2971), a Titan TD5. It continued in service until 1966, when it was sold to one of the shed men. It does not seem to have seen any further road use. Breakdown duties were then taken over by an AEC ! An ex military AEC Matador chassis was obtained and stripped down and overhauled in the Corporation's workshops. It was then sent to Pennine Coachcraft for a modern body to be fitted. This, and the third bus ever to be owned by Wigan, were the only AECs to run in the Wigan Corporation fleet.

Several other old buses ran as service vehicles: a 1920 Tilling-Stevens and a 1925 Thornycroft survived as departmental trucks, the latter being replaced by an Austin utility vehicle in 1943. Two of the 1932 TS4s remained in the ownership of the Corporation, one as a mobile library, the other as a dual-control driver training bus. This vehicle, No.81 (EK 8867) was not withdrawn until 1964, when it passed into preservation. TS7 No.15 became a mobile library for Leigh Corporation, and received the blue and cream colour scheme used at Leigh.

Contrast the lines of the Leyland lowbridge body (opposite) with the English Electric lowbridge body of No.7 (JP 3702) new in 1939, but seen here after the war having lost its gold lining out.　　　　　　　　　　　　　　　　　　(H. Wall Collection)

75 replacement buses

Wigan is one of the few towns in Great Britain to have succeeded in buying a large quantity of the vehicles of its choice to replace older units under the immediate post-war conditions of restrictions and quotas. Indeed, the 75 lowbridge Leylands that arrived in 1946-7, mainly for vehicle replacement, represented 50% of the fleet, which now became 150 strong.

All the tram and trolleybus replacement vehicles, the seven earlier TD1s and all bar four of the TD2s of 1932-3 were cleared out in a period of some 9 months. (See page 30) The new buses were in two groups, JP 5500-37 based on Titan PD1 chassis delivered between November 1946-March 1947, and JP 6000-36 based on Titan PD1A chassis delivered June-August 1947. The list below illustrates which vehicles were replaced, and the oddness of the way in which Wigan allocated its fleet numbers. Not all of the buses numbered from 129-150 were "extras", as included in this replacement scheme were the "wartime reserve" of fourteen. The unused numbers 13 and 113, and the number 65 once carried by the breakdown vehicle were brought into use.

New in 1946		New in 1947		New in 1947	
JP 5500	131	JP 5526	144	JP 6013	49
JP 5501	134	JP 5527	145	JP 6014	59
JP 5502	135	JP 5528	146	JP 6015	41
JP 5503	1	JP 5529	147	JP 6016	54
JP 5504	65	JP 5530	148	JP 6017	20
JP 5505	3	JP 5531	149	JP 6018	25
JP 5506	69	JP 5532	150	JP 6019	29
JP 5507	129	JP 5533	24	JP 6020	76
JP 5508	130	JP 5534	35	JP 6021	77
JP 5509	11	JP 5535	42	JP 6022	78
JP 5510	132	JP 5536	52	JP 6023	79
JP 5511	133	JP 5537	53	JP 6024	83
JP 5512	136			JP 6025	44
JP 5513	137	JP 6000	55	JP 6026	46
JP 5514	138	JP 6001	43	JP 6027	21
JP 5515	139	JP 6002	57	JP 6028	27
JP 5516	140	JP 6003	58	JP 6029	28
JP 5517	141	JP 6004	56	JP 6030	31
JP 5518	72	JP 6005	51	JP 6031	33
JP 5519	73	JP 6006	50	JP 6032	34
JP 5520	74	JP 6007	38	JP 6033	37
JP 5521	75	JP 6008	39	JP 6034	36
JP 5522	13	JP 6009	40	JP 6035	22
JP 5523	113	JP 6010	45	JP 6036	23
JP 5524	142	JP 6011	47		
JP 5525	143	JP 6012	48		

As disclosed on page 25, the 75 new buses were first reserved in 1942. In the meantime, Wigan was obliged to accept three Guys and three Bristols allocated by the MoWT. In April 1945, the same body allocated ten Crossley chassis to Wigan, but as lowbridge bodies were not available, there was going to be a delay in delivery. The General Manager, Mr. Brierley, who was about to retire at the end of the year, asked for a conference with the MoWT and Leyland. The latter was about to restart bus production, and Mr. Brierley wanted to press his outstanding order for 75 new buses on Leyland chassis, and avoid the need to purchase more non-standard machines.

It was not until December 1945 that a contract could be drawn up, and this was for 38 buses only. The Ministry of War Transport was still involved with the allocation of buses, and Wigan were only allowed half the number they required. However, one month later, now under the managership of Mr. J. McKnight a further contract for the remaining 37 was signed, immediately after the wartime controls of MoWT were lifted
There was still a delay, however, as Leyland had yet to reopen its bodybuilding plant.

As seen below, the new buses were an all-Leyland product, with bodywork of similar appearance and specification to the immediate pre-war standard Wigan bus. Compare the bus depicted on page 21 with the one seen in the top picture on the rear cover. When three-track route indicators became esssential, the PD1 type had one of the green marker lights replaced by a narrow aperture showing one digit only, to be used in combination with the existing number blind (again, see rear cover).

The Mount Pleasant terminus of the Wigan - Liverpool route, before it was moved to a less central "bus station" in Russell St., Liverpool.   A view of No.143 being passed by a Crosville Motor Services Bristol K6A with Strachan body, of identical design to Wigan Nos.126-128.   (Norman Forbes)

The great clear-out

The delivery of 75 new buses permitted the disposal of all remaining petrol engined double deckers together with some of the oldest with diesel engines. Had it not been for the times, all would have gone for scrap, but bus operators across the country were in dire need of machines which could be rebuilt or refurbished for a few more years service until new buses were easily available. In November 1946, **Crosville Motor Services** offered Wigan £1000 for five defective petrol engined vehicles, Nos.4A, 6A, 64A, 66A and 75. These were rebuilt by the new owner in time to enter service for the summer timetable 1947.

In December 1946, nearby **St.Helens Corporation** paid £250 each for Nos.35, 42, 63A and 67A. The price paid indicates these vehicles were also defective, because **Barton Transport** paid £2500 for six petrol engined vehicles (Nos.2A, 68A,69, 70A, 71A and 72) in a deal effected in January 1947. **Lincolnshire Road Car Company** paid £500 for two oil-engined vehicles and £400 for two petrol-engined vehicles at the same time. The buses involved were TD1s Nos. 1, 52, 62A and TD2 No.24.

Two further TD1s, Nos.11 and 73 were sold to **W. Gash & Sons,Newark** in 7/47 at £400 each. The same price was paid by **Leigh Corporation** for Nos.3 and 74, which joined the Leigh fleet as Nos.40-41, taking the numbers of TD1s which Leigh had recently sold to Crosville. All the above sales were negotiated directly with the purchasers by Wigan Corporation at the time when the first 38 Leyland PD1s were delivered.

When the second batch of 37 new buses came, 16 of the withdrawn vehicles were immediately hired to **Ribble Motor Services** for July and August 1947.(The charge, as during the war, was £25 per vehicle per month.) They worked from the Ribble garages at Wigan and Bootle. The buses involved were TD1s Nos.38-41, 43, 45, 47-50, 54-56, 76 and TD2s Nos.25 and 29. After this, there were no more sales by the Corporation to individual buyers. In October the General Manager reported that 36 surplus buses had been sold to a Manchester dealer for £7200 (i.e. £200 each)

This picture shows No.43 on hire to Ribble in July 1947, working on route L9 in Crosby, near Liverpool. Note the bus carries the Wigan and the Ribble fleetnames.

(Norman Forbes)

The first highbridge buses

In 1950, a radical innovation at Wigan was the introduction of highbridge buses. The number of low bridges in the Wigan area was decreasing, and it was now possible to work many routes with full-height double deckers. Once again Leyland received a contract to supply 30 new buses, (15 in replacement of older vehicles and 15 for fleet expansion), taking the total of Wigan buses to its maximum of 165.

The decision to order highbridge buses was confirmed in June 1947, and in September 1949 it was decided to fit three-track route number boxes (situated above the destination) to these new vehicles. Some other vehicles were later rebuilt with this style of destination equipment. The 1950 order for 30 56 seat highbridge buses on PD2/1 chassis was followed by an order in 1953 for 12 buses on PD2/12 chassis, this time built to the width of 8 feet. AEK 501-512 replaced older vehicles and were Nos. 8, 15-17, 63, 93-99.

JP 8300	151
JP 8301	152
JP 8302	153
JP 8303	154
JP 8304	155
JP 8305	156
JP 8306	157
JP 8307	158
JP 8308	159
JP 8309	160
JP 8310	161
JP 8311	162
JP 8312	12
JP 8313	14
JP 8314	19
JP 8315	26
JP 8316	30
JP 8317	32
JP 8318	84
JP 8319	85
JP 8320	86
JP 8321	87
JP 8322	88
JP 8323	89
JP 8324	90
JP 8325	91
JP 8326	163
JP 8327	164
JP 8328	165
JP 8329	92

Above a highbridge bus of the first type passes beneath the London-Glasgow line in Wallgate.   (Ron Phillips)
Below, a 1953 bus, No.16 on the Standish route (BCVMA).

Royal Tigers & Tiger Cubs

By far the oldest buses in the fleet in 1951 were the single deck Tiger TS4s, and it was time for them to be replaced. Leyland now had a single deck chassis with under-floor engine, the Royal Tiger, and Wigan took four of these with N.C.M.E. 43 seat front entrance bodies in 1951 (JP 9061-9064) and again in 1953 (AEK 513-516). The first group replaced TS4 single deckers No.18 of 1933 and Nos.80-82 of 1932, taking the same numbers. The second group took numbers 100-103, and replaced 1933 TS4s 8, 16-17 and 1936 TS7 No.15 . The fleet numbers of these single deckers passed to new double deckers, but those of double deckers 100-103 were re-used by the Royal Tigers.For a short period, the older buses in this latter group were still running along-side their double deck counterparts, and "A" was added to their numbers.

The only new bus purchased by Wigan in 1955 was a further Leyland Royal Tiger (BJP 364) No.105 which took a number made vacant in 1954 by the sale of the LT9 with that number. The other two Lion LT9s were sold in 1956 and their places filled by two Leyland Tiger Cub PSUC1/1 chassis, again with N.C.M.E. 43 seat front entrance bodies. The new 104 and 106 were registered DEK 534-535. It is interesting to note that although the Royal Tigers and Tiger Cubs in the Wigan fleet were similar in appearance, the Tiger Cubs weighed one and a half tons less. (For example, No.105 weighed 7tons 12 cwt, but Tiger Cub No.104 weighed 5 tons 19 cwt.)

All pre-war single deckers had now been replaced. An additional Tiger Cub PSU1/1, No.23 (JJP 501) with a Massey 43 seat front-entrance body was obtained in 1962 for operation with one man.

The exterior of the Central Depot is seen in this picture of Royal Tiger No.105, be-hind which can be seen another Royal Tiger, No.18 (JP 9061)   (Ron Phillips)

The Central Depot

The temporary structure in Woodhouse Lane used by the first electric trams from 1901 did not even have an office. The Tramways Department decided to build offices close to the Market Square and to have a central tram depot in Hallgate, also close to the town centre. A dispute over the Hallgate site causcd a new less central location to be chosen off Wallgate, in Melverley Street. A depot was put into use here in July 1904, but was not officially opened until June 1905. It could accommodate only standard gauge trams, and the narrow gauge cars remained at the corrugated iron shed on the Martland Mill route until they were withdrawn in 1925.

The Central Depot initially housed 53 single deck trams. As its repair facilities were very limited, the Corporation retained the former steam tram depot at Pemberton for repair and painting of car bodies, and some trams were even constructed there by Massey in 1921-2. The car shed at Melverley Street was lengthened when the standard gauge fleet was enlarged by the addition of 24 new double deck cars. This long and single ended building was used by the bus fleet from 1931: the depot shunters had to drive the vehicles in and out of the shed over the tramway pits. In 1939 an adjacent garage was built to house 92 buses, and subsequently the old tram shed was rebuilt by filling in the pits and opening up the side walls to give a "drive through" facility. An underfloor heating system was installed in both buildings.

The interior of the 1939 shed at the Central Depot in 1955. To the left is "unfrozen" Leyland TD7 no.120, with its Leyland body rebuilt with post 1950 style indicators. On the right is N.C.M.E. bodied No. 107.   (BCVMA)

Further rebuilding took place in the mid-fifties when an area between the two sheds was walled off to provide an engine overhaul shop, stores and tyre-fitting shop etc. A new block was constructed for office/mess rooms, stores, and a driver training school. For their first hands-on experience after basic training, new drivers were put behind the wheel of a bus and took the vehicle on a circular tour of the large patch of waste ground which surrounded the garage (see picture on pages 24-5). The building was passed to GMPTE in 1973, and is still used by First Manchester buses.

The Wigan Corporation Transport Offices and cash pay-in point at the Market Square forms the background to this picture of No.150 (JP 5532) in May 1947.   (BCVMA)

The Market Place offices, opened in 1905, were the nerve centre of the under-taking, and faced onto the main central terminus of the town routes. Some longer distance services, such as route 320 to Liverpool, started in the bus station behind the new Market Hall. All cash taken by conductors and drivers was handed in at this central point. In tramcar days, the current was left switched on after the last service tram had run to allow two cars, one from Melverly Street and another (narrow gauge) from Martland Mill (Woodhouse Lane) to bring the cash to town, but this practice ceased when safes were installed at the car sheds to store money overnight.

Wigan Corporation also owned depots at Pemberton (ex steam tram), used until 1920 as a repair shop and then sold to Massey Brothers, Platt Bridge (ex steam tram) used briefly as an electric car shed and later leased for other purposes, and Hindley (ex steam tram) which was later leased out.

Even parts of the Central depot and site were leased out, as the building had an area of vacant land surrounding it. On occasions, the adjacent River Douglas burst its banks, so pumps were provided to clear water from the main depot. In the early days trams were sometimes immobilised by the flood water.

New-Look Titans

The five double deckers delivered in 1956 were mounted on the Leyland Titan PD2/20 chassis with a full-width bonnet structure replacing the exposed radiator of the PD2/12 model. The bodies were built by N.C.M.E., and were of 5 bay all-metal construction with 58 seats. Registered CEK 837-41, the new buses took fleet numbers 114,119 and 123-5. The following year nine more similar buses were purchased. Nos.2, 4, and 6 (DEK 105-7) had Massey 58 seat bodies, and Nos.107-112 (DEK 113/108-112) had N.C.M.E. 59 seat bodies. It is curious to note that Nos. 108-112 actually carried registration numbers matching the fleet numbers !

The final vehicles of this type, to the updated PD2/30 specification, arrived in 1958. Bodied by Massey with 61 seats and rear platform doors and heaters, were Nos.7, 9, 10 (DJP 751-753), intended for the Liverpool service. Six more by N.C.M.E. with 61 seats and open platforms, were to be the last Wigan double deck buses without doors, and took numbers 115-118, 126-127 (DJP 754-759).

No.119 (CEK 838) is an N.C.M.E.bodied Leyland PD2/20. It is photographed in Station Road, by Wigan Central, in which a train can be seen in this mid-sixties view.
(Ron Phillips)

A number of Wigan buses of this type were sold to Widnes (Halton Borough Transport). This picture at Widnes Town Hall shows DJP 752 (ex No. 9, with platform doors) passing a Halton Leyland Leopard.
(Ron Phillips)

Passengers board a Massey bodied front entrance Wigan Corporation bus at Platt Bridge. The use of front entrance buses meant that some stop signs (positioned for rear entrance buses) were badly sited. Here the bus blocks the exit from a minor road which is named "TRAM STREET" It was the entrance to the former Platt Bridge steam tram depot. The building survived for many years under Corporation owner-ship, but was rented to an industrial tenant. (Ron Phillips)

Leyland Tiger Cub 104 on route 333 is seen at the Bus Station. Services operated jointly with Ribble Motor Services commenced here. (Ron Phillips)

Front-Entrance Double Deckers

The British bus manufacturers introduced new models in the late fifties, rear-engined double deckers, with up to 78 seats, and longer traditional front-engined buses with up to 73 seats. The latter could be fitted with a front entrance, safeguarded by doors, or the traditional rear platform entrance as hitherto used in Wigan.

When placing orders for delivery in 1959, Wigan chose the 30 feet long version of the Leyland Titan PD3/2, which introduced Wigan bus drivers to the "Pneumo-cyclic" gearbox. This air-operated gearbox was controlled by a small selector lever and dispensed with the traditional clutch pedal. The bodywork order was divided between Massey and Northern Counties, the former building four (Nos.5, 60-2) and the latter constructing six (Nos.64-8, 128). Registration numbers were EJP 501-10.

These new buses had front doors, and although each coachbuilder will have been given a similar specification, the Massey bodies had 72 seats and the Northern Counties ones had 69. Despite this, and a different external profile, the two types were only one hundredweight different in weight (Massey at 8.9.1.; N.C.M.E. at 8.8.1.)

The following year both coachbuilders built six similar vehicles, but this time all had 70 seats and the weight difference was one and a half hundredweight. Massey bodied Nos.1, 137-8 (GJP 8-10) and Nos.141/3/4 (GJP 17-9) and Northern Counties provided Nos.120-2, 129, 134/5 (GJP 11-16).

Massey bodied Leyland PD3/2 No.60 on a January day at the Abbey Lakes terminus. It was from here that Wigan's last tram departed and it was here that an official picture of a Leyland Titan TD1 was taken to mark the changeover to buses. The conductor is seen on the left walking towards the departure stop, probably to chat with the crew of a standing bus.   (Ron Phillips)

St. Helens Fronts

It was neighbouring St. Helens Corporation which persuaded Leyland Motors to revise the full width frontal design of half-cab double deckers to a form which was more "user-friendly" for both driver and maintenance staff. Making extensive use of glass fibre, the new front first appeared in 1960 on St.Helens Corporation buses Nos. K172-9 (LDJ 982-89), which were designated type PD2A/30. Wigan adopted the new fronts for the third batch of PD3 chassis. These were designated PD3A/2, and four-teen, all with 70 seats, were delivered in 1961, with the usual arrangement for supply of bodywork: i.e. equal numbers from the two local makers. Nos. 57-9 (HEK 705-7) and Nos.39, 40, 42, 49 (HJP 1-4) had Massey bodies, and Nos. 51, 54, 70, 71, 74, 77, 79 (HJP 5-11) had Northern Counties.

The larger buses were, of course, deployed on the busiest routes, but were not essential on the quieter services. For 1962 it was decided to specify the shorter PD2 type chassis, with front doors, synchromesh transmission, the fibre-glass fronts , and 64 seats. The chassis type was PD2A/27 .For 1962, eight such chassis, with bodywork divided equally between Masssey and Northern Counties, were registered JJP 502-509, and took Nos. 35-7, 143 (Massey) and 130-33 (N.C.M.E.) Additionally, a Tiger Cub PSUC1/1 No.21 (JJP 501) was acquired for operation with one man. The new double deckers were, of course, operated by a driver and a conductor.

For 1963, an order for 12 more PD2A/27 chassis was placed, and again the bodywork was divided equally between the two local coachbuilders. Nos.41/3-5/7-8 (KEK 739-44) had Massey bodies, and Nos.52, 55-6, 69, 75-6 (KEK 745-50) carried Northern Counties bodies. The following year there was an order for 10, all with bodies by Massey, but delivered in two batches in September and December, which points to the fact that Northern Counties had been unable to accept the work to body chassis on time, and Massey had therefore filled the breech. Nos.146-50 were the first group and Nos.3, 11, 24, 29, 31 were the second, carrying registrations AEK 1-10B. Several future groups of Wigan buses received registration numbers commencing at 1 and from 1969 there was even an attempt to group fleet numbers into a less random sequence than hitherto.

As will be seen, the next two orders for new buses were also for 64 seat front-entrance half-cab types, but the country-wide drive for one man operation and new government legislation concerning the design of buses and tied to a system by which the cost of new buses was partially met by government (Bus Grant Scheme) caused Leyland Motors to cease the manufacture of the Titan model. Wigan was now forced to move away from the "traditional" kind of bus. The Wigan fleet had already become much more diverse than it ever had been. From 1929-1938 all the double deckers had been to a similar design, whichever make of body was carried. From 1939-1953 only standard Leyland metal-framed bodies had been used, wartime excepted. By the mid-sixties, each new batch of buses was distinctly different, although the well established livery preserved the family resemblance.

Falling Traffic

This book is about Wigan buses, not the routes and services, but like most bus operators Wigan had been carrying progressively less passengers since a peak in 1953, when 61,062,964 passengers were carried. Less passengers meant less revenue, and amongst other things a need for less buses. By 1967, the number of persons carried had fallen to 42,570,519. No new buses were purchased in 1965, and only eight were purchased in 1966-7. The fleet strength in 1967 was 151, having fallen from its peak of 165, and the overall total continued to fall. At the end of 1968, ten buses were sold to a dealer without replacement, while another was declared a total write-off after being hit by a lorry whilst parked at Horwich in 1967.

Falling traffic affected manufacturers as well as bus operators. Through the sixties, the General Manager had maintained the policy of ordering Leyland chassis first, and then discussing the bodywork later. Leyland Motors were experiencing some problems with re-organisation and mergers in the late sixties and early seventies, and Wigan found it necessary to order chassis well in advance to avoid delays in delivery. The shrinking market for bus bodies led to the closure of the Massey works, and from 1969 Wigan had only one local bodybuilder, Northern Counties. Greater Manchester Passenger Transport Executive, which took over Wigan buses in 1974, continued to support this firm, and it survived independently until it was taken over by Plaxton. It now forms part of a larger group, and buses are still built in Wigan.

The St. Helens fibre glass front is seen on No.69 (KEK 748), a Leyland PD2A/27 with Northern Counties front entrance body. The bus is descending Wallgate en route for Marus Bridge. (Ron Phillips)

The last Leyland Titans

It was a sign of the times that when the Transport Committee met in June 1966 they ordered nine new Titans, but only six were delivered. The cancelled trio were replaced by two single deckers (see next page). This was the result of the falling traffic and the need to introduce one man operation.

The six Titans reverted to having exposed radiators. By this period the demand for half-cab buses had fallen so sharply that Leyland had reduced the range of options. Two of the 1966 order were delivered in December of that year as Nos.139-40, with registrations DEK 2-3D and Massey bodywork. Even this had changed and was less curvaceous than hitherto and more akin to the Northern Counties design. The other four were 72, 73, 78 and 113, with registrations DEK 4-7E.....note the change of suffix as they were delivered in 1967.

The final delivery of Titans was ordered later in 1967, with N.C.M.E. bodies. The chassis were the 8369th - 8376th PD2 type Titans to be made by Leyland, and only six more for Darwen Corporation were to be built. They were registered FEK 1-9F and were numbered 25-28, 32-4, 38 and 46. Some of the longer PD3 type chassis were still to come for other operators, but in 1969 the very last Leyland Titan PD3 left the factory.

The first of the Massey bodied PD2/37 Titans with exposed radiator, (DEK 2D) of December 1966 carries fleet number 139 and a slightly revised livery: same colours but with "County Borough of Wigan" and the coat of arms between decks. (H.Wall)

The Panther Cubs

The Leyland Panther Cub was a very rare breed - less than one hundred were built. Manchester Corporation is said to have inspired the model: a medium capacity city bus made by putting together a low-level Panther chassis (see page 43) with the less powerful O.400 engine of the Tiger Cub range instead of the O.600 or the O.680 of the heavier Leyland models. It was not a success as it weighed almost as much as its big brother, the Panther. A few operators, including Manchester, found the Panther Cub a troublesome machine, although the Wigan examples are said to have worked well enough. Ironically, they ended up after 1974 with Greater Manchester P.T.E., whose predecessor had rejected the model.

Wigan had just two, model PSRC1/1, with Massey 43 seat dual door bodies.The use of two doors, one at the front for passengers to board and pay the driver, and one in the middle for use by passengers wishing to alight, made these two buses much more convenient for one man operation on busy town services. Apart from the nine Titans of 1968, all future Wigan buses would have two doors.

Wigan Corporation Panther Cub No.20 (DJP 468E) is seen here in service in Malta where it ended up after sale by GMPTE. It has now been "rescued" and brought back to Britain for restoration and continued preservation.   (M.Fenton)

Wigan's Panther Cubs were allocated No.20 (DJP 468E) and No.22 (EEK 1F). The photograph shows the restrained styling of the Massey bodies, whose handsome appearance was contrary to the harsh "modern" styling applied by some coachbuilders to the stepped chassis frame, which allowed the forward part of the vehicle to be low while the rearward part had to rise up to cover the engine and transmission.

41

First rear engined double deckers

The Leyland Atlantean in its production form first appeared in 1958, at the Commercial Motor Show. It was not until ten years later that Wigan's first example of this model was exhibited at the Show, in the form of bus No.166, (FJP 566G) the first of a batch of ten. The remaining nine which entered service in 1969 were allocated Nos.157-165 (GJP 2-10G), and had Northern Counties 71 seat dual door bodies.The chassis were of the PDR1A/1 type, essentially an improved version of the model that had been introduced ten years earlier, and which was shortly to be replaced by a new range.

166 was the highest number ever allocated to a Wigan bus, but of course by this time the fleet had been reduced from the peak figure of 165 and the use of 166 was "symbolic". The Atlanteans represented a radical change: not only the first rear-engined double deckers in Wigan, but the first double deckers with two doors and the first intended for one man operation.

Curiously, in the same year as the largest buses so far used by Wigan entered service, a 19 seat coach on a Bedford chassis was purchased for use as a committee vehicle. This was, by 1969, a rather outdated adjunct to a municipal bus undertaking, although such vehicles (trams and buses) had been a feature of many undertakings in pre-war times. The Bedford was not used in normal passenger service, and was not confined to work for the transport department, but was used by other council services.It was allocated number 92P (the "P" presumably indicated "petrol"), and was kept at the Central Garage. By this time, over 60 other vehicles belonging to the council were being maintained by the transport department workshops.

As the years went by, the Wigan Corporation transport undertaking was having change forced upon it, and the process was accelerating. Under the stable management of Mr. Brierley (pre 1946) and Mr. McKnight, vehicle policy had been conservative to say the least. From the mid-fifties, each batch of new vehicles took one step forward with regard to innovation, but as the sixties progressed, the steps increased. The first Atlanteans, the Panther Cubs and the Panthers were radical innovations. Despite this the look of Wigan buses was preserved. The livery had changed slightly, with the gradual dropping of gold lining on the carmine red and the thin red lining out on the white, and variations in the style and shape of the fleet numbers. But it was still re-markable to see white roofs on buses new in the seventies.

The writer recalls his earliest impression of Wigan buses, when as a child he was taken each week to a butchers shop at Old Swan, Liverpool. Here could be seen a constant stream of trams and buses of Liverpool Corporation, in a drab wartime garb of olive green and khaki. The cream used by Liverpool had been painted over to avoid attention from enemy aircraft. Once in a while, a Wigan Corporation bus would pass by, working on the joint service to its home town, a vision of red and gold and white, a Leyland amongst a sea of AECs. It was the white and gold which was so special.

The Panthers

In July 1968 the Committee resolved to purchase twelve single deck Leyland PSUR1/1 Panther chassis, at a cost of £3,358 each (compare this price with the cost of the previous double deck Atlanteans at £3,383 each.) Before confirming the order, a trial was made during August with a 36 foot long demonstration Panther. Of course, the Atlanteans had not yet arrived, and there was little experience with high capacity double or single deckers in the transport department. The order for the Panthers was confirmed by the end of the year, with an amended price of £3,443 per bus. The bodywork order was placed in January 1969 with Northern Counties.

The Panther was a low level chassis which allowed for a lower than hitherto step level at the front entrance and central exit doorways. Aft of the central door, the chassis cranked upwards to allow for an underfloor mounted engine and transmission. As on the Atlantean, gearchanges were operated pneumatically by the flick of a lever.

The llustration shows the design of this chassis, first introduced in 1964 by Leyland, and also used by AEC for its Swift model. At the front can be seen the radiator, which was positioned here to maximise cooling, the steering column, and hand brake. the gear control is attached to the steering column. The chassis is then straight for over half the length of the vehicle before rising up for the attachment of the rear springs and driving axle. Then comes the gearbox and the "flat" (or horizontal) engine. The part seen rising at the rear is the coolant reservoir.

The weaknesses of the Panther are apparent: the weight of the engine and transmission are all behind the rear axle, so that there are stresses placed on the chassis frame and bodywork just ahead of the axle. It is also difficult for mechanics to work on the engine and transmission when they are housed so compactly beneath the floor and are liable to be covered in road dirt.

The advantage of the Panther was its ease of control and ability to handle a large number of passengers with one man in charge. When they were ordered, cost-cutting was essential, and the introduction of one man operation of buses was soon to be almost universal in Great Britain. The Panther, which with standing passengers could carry over 60 persons, was regarded as a better option than large capacity double deckers, as the driver could see the people in the whole of the vehicle.

Above is an illustration of the Leyland Panther badge, an optional extra which was not fitted by all customers. The photograph below shows the plain front worn by Wigan No.83, which carries no indication of the vehicle make. Behind the plain mesh grille is a radiator to cool the rear mounted engine, for which the access hatch may just be seen

The livery is much simplified, the lower half carmine red, the upper half white. A curiosity is the variety of lights on the front: green marker lights, headlamps and spot lamps, side lights combined with traffic indicators and a PAY ON ENTRY sign to remind passengers that the bus is one man operated. Finally, the roller blind indicators would also be illuminated.

Wigan Panther No.83 with Northern Counties bodywork shows the higher level of the rear side windows and simplified livery style.   (photo courtesy H.Wall)

Wigan's Last Buses

It is curious that the final buses purchased by Wigan should be the largest, as they came when traffic levels, as has already been said, were falling. Of course, traffic managers in those days were becoming adept at restructuring many well established services to let one bus do the work of two at peak times and run part empty at others. For 1971 delivery an order was placed for the long version of the Atlantean (PDR2/1) with Northern Counties 79 seat dual door bodies. As with the Panthers 80-91, groups of convenient blank numbers were allocated: 92-97 and 151-156 (KJP 20-31J). These buses entered service in April 1971.

The final buses in Wigan livery entered service in July 1972. Again 79 seat Atlanteans, these were of the new breed, the AN68. Leyland introduced a new form of nomenclature for its models in the seventies, the initial letters indicating the model, the figures representing the engine, in this case the O.680. The Wigan examples were of the 10 metre long type, AN68/2R. There were numerous improvements over the early design, and this model became a best-seller, and was only killed off by legislation. The last Atlanteans new in Britain were delivered in 1984. For the first and only time, in order to allocate these ten buses a complete block of numbers, in fact 1-10, three buses were **renumbered** and placed in a group with their fellows.

No. 1 (GJP 8) of 1960 was renumbered 136, forming a group with 137-8

No. 5 (EJP 501) of 1959 was renumbered 63, forming a group with 60-2

No. 9 (AEK 6B) of 1964 was renumbered 30, forming a group with 29 & 31

The final Atlanteans, illustrated in the lower picture on the rear cover, were similar in appearance to the 1971 delivery but for the detail of the windscreen and front panel. The 1971 PDR2/1s had curved windscreen glasses and a different arrangement of headlamps and spotlamps from the AN68/2Rs of 1973 which had flat screens as did the Panthers. Nos.1-10 were registered NEK 1-10K.

There is now a strange irony to relate. Wigan Corporation ordered six more single deck buses which were delivered new to GMPTE and they were **not Leylands !** They were technically ordered from the Leyland organisation, which had taken over the Bristol based bus factory of Bristol Commercial Vehicles and were of the medium-sized Bristol LH series. These were to be fitted with 43 seat front entrance bodies by Eastern Coach Works. In fact, these vehicles entered service after Wigan Corporation had ceased to exist, from 1st April 1974. They were registered BNE 763-8H by the Greater Manchester Passenger Transport Executive (GMPTE), and took the fleet numbers 1320-5.

And so it ended. Of course, most of the vehicles of Wigan Corporation remained at the Central Depot and saw out their working lives there. Yet another loyal Leyland customer had ceased trading.

45

This picture of a Wigan Leyland with a Northern Counties all-metal lowbridge body perhaps epitomises municipal transport in the 1930s. The vehicle is number 108 (JP 3701).   (photo courtesy H. Wall)

SUMMARY OF LEYLAND BUS ORDERS

Date	Registration Nos.	Type	Bodywork	Total	Page Ref.
1927	EK 6042-6043	PLSC1	Leyland	2	4, 6, 19, **24**
1928	EK 6281	PLSC1	Leyland	1	4, 6, 19, **24**
1929	EK 7260-3	TD1	Leyland	4	**8, 24**
1930	EK 7434-6	TD1	Leyland	3	8, **9**, 24
	EK 7906-14	TD1	Leyland	9	10-11
1931	EK 8039-44	TD1	Leyland	6	10-11
	EK 8086-91	TD1	NC/My/Ss	6	10-11
	EK 8100-16	TD1	NC/My/Ss	17	10-11
	EK 8330-3	TD1	Leyland	4	12
1932	EK 8866-8	TS4	Santus	3	13
	EK 8669-78	TD2	NCME	10	13
1933	EK 9309-12	TS4	Santus/My	4	**15**. 16, 17
	EK 9313-22	TD2	NCME	10	16, 17
1936	JP 1211-2	TD4	NCME	2	16
	JP 1213	TS7	Santus	1	16
	JP 1925-7	TD4	NCME	3	ccccc
1937	JP 2025-31	TD4	NC/Massey	7	18
	JP 2195-6	TD4	NC/Massey	2	18
1938	JP 2965-72	TD5	NC/Massey	8	19
	JP 3533-5	LT9	NCME	3	19, **20**
1939	JP 3700-1	TD5	NCME	2	19, **33, 46**
	JP 3702-4	TD5	English Electric	3	19, **27**
	JP 3705-7	TD5	Leyland	3	19
	JP 3900-6	TD5	Leyland	7	19
1940	JP 4700-13	TD7	Leyland	14	21
1942	JP 4816-7	TD7	Leyland	2	23, **26**
	JP 4922	TD7	E.Lancs	1	24
1945	JP 5130-5	Utility Guys			25-6
	JP 5133-5	Utility Bristols			25-6
1946	JP 5500-37	PD1	Leyland	38	28, **29, 34**
1947	JP 6000-36	PD1A	Leyland	37	28
1950	JP 8300-29	PD2/1	Leyland	30	**31**
1952	JP 9061-4	PSU1/13	NCME	4	32
1953	AEK 501-12	PD2/12	Leyland	12	**31**
	AEK 513-15	PSU1/13	NCME	3	32
1955	BJP 364	PSU1/13	NCME	1	**32**
1956	CEK 837-41	PD2/20	NCME	5	35
1957	DEK 105-7	PD2/20	Massey	3	35
	DEK 108-13	PD2/20	NCME	6	35
	DEK 534-5	PSUC1/1	NCME	2	35, **36**
1958	DJP 751-3	PD2/30	Massey	3	**35**
	DJP 754-9	PD2/30	NCME	6	35
1959	EJP 501-5	PD3/2	Massey	5	**37**
	EJP 506-10	PD3/2	NCME	5	37

continued overleaf

Leyland Fleet Series - Wigan Corporation

Date	Registration Nos.	Type	Bodywork	Total	Page Ref.
1960	GJP 8-10	PD3/2	Massey	3	37
	GJP 11-16	PD3/2	NCME	6	37
	GJP 17-19	PD3/2	Massey	3	37
1961	HEK 705-7	PD3A/2	Massey	3	38
	HJP 1-4	PD3A/2	Massey	4	38
	HJP 5-11	PD3A/2	NCME	7	38
1962	JJP 501	PSUC1/1	Massey	1	38
	JJP 502-5	PD2A/27	Massey	4	38
	JJP 506-9	PD2A/27	NCME	4	38
1963	KEK 739-50	PD2A/27	Massey	6	38
	KEK 745-50	PD2A/27	NCME	6	38, **39**
1964	AEK 1-5B	PD2A/27	Massey	5	38
	AEK 6-10B	PD2A/27	Massey	5	38
1966	DEK 2-3D	PD2/37	Massey	2	**40**
1967	DEK 4-7E	PD2/37	NCME	4	40
	DJP 468E	PSRC1/1	Massey	1	**41**
	EEK 1F	PSRC1/1	Massey	1	41
1968	FEK 1-9F	PD2/37	Massey	9	40
	FJP 566G	PDR1A/1	NCME	1	42
1969	GJP 2-10G	PDR1A/1	NCME	9	42
1970	HJP 950-61H	PSUR1A/1R	NCME	12	43, **44**
1971	KJP 20-31J	PDR2/1	NCME	12	45
1972	NEK 1-10K	AN68/2R	NCME	10	45

Bold figures denote an illustration

Abbreviations used in this book

BCVMA   British Commercial Vehicle Museum Archive, Leyland
GMPTE   Greater Manchester Passenger Transport Executive
NCME   Northern Counties Motor & Engineering Company, Wigan